United States Government Accountability Office

Report to Congressional Committees

I0448740

September 2013

PUBLIC TRANSIT

Transit Agencies' Use of Contracting to Provide Service

GAO Highlights

Highlights of GAO-13-782, a report to congressional committees

PUBLIC TRANSIT

Transit Agencies' Use of Contracting to Provide Service

Why GAO Did This Study

Some transit agencies have found that they can save money by contracting out some or all of their services with private providers, while others have found it more beneficial to use their own staff to provide services. The Moving Ahead for Progress in the 21st Century Act mandated that GAO review issues related to transit contracting. In this report, GAO identified: (1) the extent that public transit agencies contract operations and reasons why agencies decide to do so, (2) methods used to select and oversee contracted services, and (3) potential benefits, challenges, and disadvantages of contracting out public transit operations and other services.

GAO conducted a web-based survey of 637 transit agencies that submit reports to the Department of Transportation (DOT) and obtained 463 responses for a 73 percent response rate. The survey and results can be found at GAO-13-824SP. In addition, GAO interviewed federal officials, representatives from industry organizations, and national union officials. GAO also interviewed officials from 10 transit agencies, chosen based on a variety of characteristics, including geographic diversity, population served, use of contracting, and modes operated. At each transit location, GAO interviewed private transit providers, citizens' advisory groups, and local unions. The results of the survey and interviews are not generalizeable to all transit agencies. GAO also reviewed relevant studies and literature on transit contracting.

GAO is not making recommendations in this report. DOT and Department of Labor reviewed a draft of this report and had no comments.

View GAO-13-782. For more information, contact David J.Wise at (202) 512-2834 or wised@gao.gov.

What GAO Found

Contracting is a prevalent means of providing transit services. About 61 percent of the 463 transit agencies responding to GAO's survey reported they contract out some or all operations and services, while the rest reported that they do not contract out at all. According to GAO's survey, paratransit (services for the disabled), demand response (also known as dial-a-ride), and commuter rail service are most often contracted out, and fixed-route bus, heavy rail, and light rail service are most often operated by the transit agency. Operations are most frequently contracted out, followed by maintenance services. Transit agencies most consistently cite reducing costs as a factor influencing their decision to contract. Contracting can reduce costs because contractors' workforces are more flexible, with more employees working in part-time positions, and lower insurance costs, among other things. Transit agencies also frequently cited starting new service, improving efficiency, and allowing for more flexible service as reasons for contracting. State laws are generally not a reason for contracting, according to GAO's survey. Transit agencies that do not contract most often cited one of these three reasons: desire to maintain control over operations, no reason to change from the transit agency's providing service, or contracting was determined not to be cost effective.

Transit agencies GAO surveyed use various methods to select contractors and oversee contractor performance. To select contractors, most agencies used competition with a request for proposals. For oversight, transit agencies most commonly used periodic reports or meetings, on-site inspections, performance metrics, and real time monitoring, according to GAO's survey and interviews. About 84 percent of surveyed transit agencies that contract out services reported having a specific oversight unit. Of the nine transit agencies GAO interviewed that use contracting, seven used transit agency staff for monitoring, while two used contractors to perform this function. Seven of these agencies used performance metrics to establish incentives and/or penalties in contracts.

Transit agencies and contractors cited benefits and challenges to contracting, while labor unions primarily noted disadvantages—most notably, reduced wages and benefits and a potential decline in safety and service, among other issues. Specifically, transit agencies GAO interviewed and the literature cited benefits to contracting, which vary based on the individual needs and circumstances of transit agencies. For example, transit agencies that use contractors view contracting as advantageous when starting or expanding services in order to avoid start-up costs—such as the large capital cost of acquiring new vehicles and hiring new staff. Contractors reported they could improve transit agencies' operational efficiency by providing the latest technologies, such as routing systems and lower costs by providing more affordable insurance on vehicles. Transit agencies also cited some challenges to contracting, such as the agency's loss of direct control over operations. Officials from national and local unions GAO spoke with said that while contracting may provide some short-term cost savings to transit agencies, in their view the savings are almost entirely from lower wages and benefits paid by the private companies to employees.

_____ United States Government Accountability Office

Contents

Abbreviations

ADA	Americans with Disabilities Act of 1990
ATU	Amalgamated Transit Union
DART	Dallas Area Rapid Transit
FTA	Federal Transit Administration
MAP-21	Moving Ahead for Progress in the 21st Century Act
METRA	Chicago Metropolitan Rail Authority
RLA	Railway Labor Act
RTA	Nashville Regional Transportation Authority
RTD	Denver Regional Transportation District
TWU	Transport Workers Union
WMATA	Washington Metropolitan Area Transit Authority

View GAO-13-824SP Key Components

Public Transit: Survey of Public Transit Agency Officials on Contracting Out Public Transit Operations and Other Services (GAO-13-824SP), an e-supplement to GAO-13-782.

September 26, 2013

The Honorable Tim Johnson
Chairman
The Honorable Mike Crapo
Ranking Member
Committee on Banking, Housing, and Urban Affairs
United States Senate

The Honorable Bill Shuster
Chairman
The Honorable Nick J. Rahall, II
Ranking Member
Committee on Transportation and Infrastructure
House of Representatives

Millions of passengers use transit services on a daily basis in the United States, and many of the local transit agencies that provide these services receive federal funding. To meet the needs of these passengers in a challenging economy, transit agencies need to use federal and other resources wisely, while also ensuring quality and safe service. Some transit agencies have found that they can save money by contracting out some or all of their services with private contractors, while others have found it more beneficial to use their own staff to provide services.

The Moving Ahead for Progress in the 21st Century Act (MAP-21) mandated that GAO report on a number of issues related to transit contracting to the House Committee on Transportation and Infrastructure and the Senate Committee on Banking, Housing, and Urban Affairs.[1] In this report, we identify (1) the extent that transit agencies contract public transit operations and services and reasons for doing so, (2) methods transit agencies use to select and oversee contracted services, and (3) potential benefits, challenges, and disadvantages of contracting out public transit operations and other services.

To determine the extent transit agencies contract public transit operations and other services, the factors they consider when deciding to contract,

---

[1]Pub. L. No. 112-141, § 20013, 126 Stat. 405, 693-694 (July 6, 2012).

and the methods used to select contractors, we surveyed all 637 transit agencies that reported to the Federal Transit Administration's (FTA) National Transit Database in 2011 and that operate fixed-route bus; demand response; the Americans with Disabilities Act of 1990 (ADA) paratransit; and/or heavy, light, or commuter rail service. We received responses from 463 transit agencies for a response rate of 73 percent.[2] Estimates and responses to survey questions in this report refer only to the views of the respondents. The survey was a census and we did not try to extrapolate the findings to the agencies that chose not to respond. For further information on our survey, see appendix I. We also interviewed FTA officials responsible for maintaining the National Transit Database to gather information about the type of information collected about transit contracting. To provide additional insight on the reasons transit agencies decide to contract, methods they use to select and oversee contracted services, and potential benefits, challenges, and disadvantages of contracting out public transit operations and other services, we interviewed officials from 10 transit agencies. We judgmentally selected these transit agencies to provide a range of geographic locations, populations served, transit modes, agency sizes, and contracting practices. At each location, we interviewed private transit contractors, citizens' advisory groups, and local unions.[3] The interviews from these locations are not generalizable to all transit agencies. In addition, we interviewed officials from the American Public Transportation Association, Community Transportation Association of America, and national labor unions representing operators and maintenance workers, as well as Federal Railroad Administration officials regarding their oversight role for commuter rail services. We also performed a literature review of transit contracting studies and articles. Further details on our scope and methodology can be found in appendix I.

We conducted this performance audit from October 2012 to September 2013 in accordance with generally accepted government auditing standards. Those standards require that we plan and perform the audit to obtain sufficient, appropriate evidence to provide a reasonable basis for

---

[2]Responses to that survey are found in GAO-13-824SP (e-supplement).

[3]Some locations did not have an active citizens' advisory group, so we could not interview its members. In some cases, the same private provider served more than one of the transit agencies that we selected for interviews. In these cases, we interviewed each private transit provider once and obtained their views related to their contracts nationwide.

our findings and conclusions based on our audit objectives. We believe that the evidence obtained provides a reasonable basis for our findings and conclusions based on our audit objectives.

Background

Transit agencies provide transportation services in a variety of ways. For purposes of this report, we used the following descriptions of transportation modes:

- **Fixed-route bus service:** rubber-tired passenger vehicles operate on fixed routes and schedules over roadways. Diesel, gasoline, battery, or alternative fuel engines power vehicles. This category also includes bus rapid transit, commuter bus, and trolley bus.

- **ADA paratransit:** vehicles operate in response to calls or requests from passengers. It uses buses, vans, or taxis to provide complementary ADA paratransit service for individuals with disabilities who are unable to use a fixed-route system. These services are associated with or attributed to ADA compliance requirements.[4]

- **Demand response (also referred to as dial-a-ride):** vehicles operate in response to calls or requests from passengers. Demand response uses small buses, vans, or taxis to provide transportation service that is not on a fixed route or schedule. For example, transportation may be provided for individuals whose access may be limited, or whose disability or health condition prevents them from using the regular fixed-route bus service. For purposes of this report, we have defined these services as unrelated to ADA requirements.

- **Commuter rail:** vehicles operate along electric or diesel-propelled railways and provide train service for local, short distance trips between a central city and adjacent suburbs.[5]

---

[4]Paratransit service is defined in Department of Transportation regulations as "comparable transportation service required by the ADA for individuals with disabilities who are unable to use fixed route transportation systems." 49 C.F.R § 37.3.

[5]Commuter rail operations are covered under the Railway Labor Act (RLA). Special bargaining dispute resolution procedures applicable to publicly owned and operated rail commuter carriers were added in 1981. 45 U.S.C. § 159a. The RLA is administered by the National Mediation Board, an independent federal agency.

- **Heavy rail:** vehicles operate on electric railways with high-volume traffic capacity. This mode has separated rights-of-way, sophisticated signaling, high platform loading and high-speed rapid-acceleration rail cars operating singly or in multi-car trains on fixed rails.

- **Light rail:** vehicles operate on electric railways with light-volume traffic capacity. The mode may have either shared or exclusive rights-of-way, low or high platform loading, or single or double car trains.

The transit contracting industry in the United States is characterized by a few large providers that operate nationwide, some mid-size regional providers, and numerous small, local providers that primarily operate bus, demand response, and ADA paratransit service. Transit agencies can contract out various aspects of their operations with contractors, such as operating the service, vehicles, maintenance, security, and administrative services. Contracting arrangements can range from the transit agency's contracting out all aspects of its operations, as is the case for a delegated management contract, to contracting out only one component of operations, such as maintenance.

The federal government has a limited role in overseeing transit contracting. FTA tracks transit agencies' contracting practices through reports submitted by transit agencies to the National Transit Database. Additionally, FTA oversees transit contracting, along with other aspects of transit agencies' operations, through procurement reviews and triennial reviews that focus on whether transit agencies have followed federal regulations and have appropriate systems in place for contracting, among other things. The Federal Railroad Administration oversees commuter rail operations but does not conduct any reviews of contracting practices. The Department of Labor is responsible for issuing what is commonly referred to as "Section 13(c)" certifications, which certify that fair and equitable labor protection arrangements are in place for employees who may be affected by certain grants of federal financial assistance.[6] When existing transit service is contracted out, Section 13(c) protections may be triggered, including assurances of employment and priority of reemployment. According to officials at the Department of Labor, after a

---

[6]When federal funds are used to acquire, improve, or operate a transit system, federal law requires arrangements to protect the rights of affected transit employees. 49 U.S.C. § 5333(b). These arrangements must be approved by the Department of Labor before FTA can release funds to grantees. The terms and conditions of the protective arrangements are included in the grantee's agreement with FTA.

search of their records and to the best of their knowledge, there has never been an instance where a transit agency has been unable to contract out public transit operations and other services because doing so would jeopardize Section 13(c) certification from the Department of Labor.

Contracting Is a Prevalent Means of Providing Transit Services

Extent of Contracting

Contracting is a prevalent means of providing transit services, with about 61 percent of the 463 transit agencies that responded to our survey reporting they contract out some aspect of their operations. By size of agency, 52 percent of small agencies, 69 percent of medium agencies, and 92 percent of large agencies had at least one service that they contracted out.[7]

According to our survey, among the agencies providing such services, paratransit, demand response, and commuter rail are more likely to be contracted out, and fixed-route bus, heavy rail, and light rail are most often operated by the transit agency. Among the approximately 61 percent of surveyed agencies that reported contracting, more agencies reported contracting for ADA paratransit than for any other service. Results from our survey shows that of 359 respondents that provide ADA paratransit services, 204, or 57 percent, contract out this service. Seven of the 10 transit agencies we interviewed also contract out ADA paratransit services. (See fig. 1.)

---

[7]We defined small agencies as those serving a population less than or equal to 200,000, medium agencies as those serving a population between 200,001 and 1,000,000, and large agencies as those serving a population greater than 1,000,000.

Figure 1: Number of Surveyed Transit Agencies That Do and Do Not Contract Services, by Mode

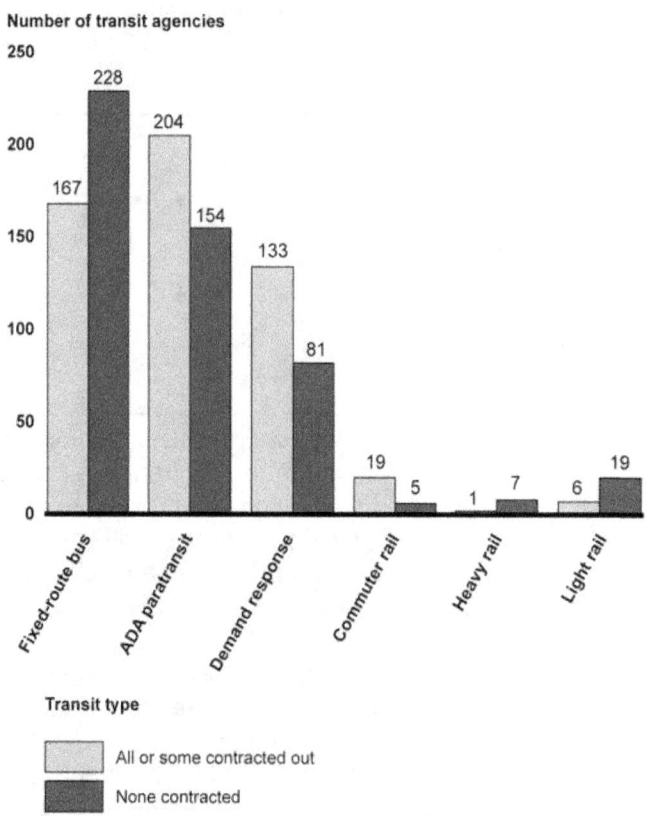

Number of transit agencies

Transit type	All or some contracted out	None contracted
Fixed-route bus	167	228
ADA paratransit	204	154
Demand response	133	81
Commuter rail	19	5
Heavy rail	1	7
Light rail	6	19

Source: GAO survey, April 2013.

Note: The numbers in this figure and the rest of the tables and figures throughout the report refer to the number of transit agencies that responded to a particular question and may not be consistent throughout the report. For example, 396 transit agencies indicated that they provide fixed-route bus service, but only 395 responded to the question about whether or not they contract out service.

Interviewees report that contracting ADA paratransit occurs for various reasons, including the following:

- ADA paratransit requires specialized training and equipment that can be difficult to provide because agencies may lack staff, expertise, or resources needed to train workers, according to a transit agency official we interviewed.

- Contracting for this service can be more cost effective than providing the service in-house. According to an industry group we spoke with, ADA paratransit operations are very expensive and for agencies, contracting this service is viewed as a way to potentially save money.

- Contracting ADA paratransit allows agencies to remove themselves from the day-to-day operations and reduces the risk and liability associated with operational responsibility, according to another transit agency official we interviewed.

We found the extent that surveyed transit agencies contract varies by type of service, but among transit agencies that contract out, operations are most often contracted across all modes, followed by maintenance services. (See table 1.)

Table 1: Of Transit Agencies That Contract, Percentage That Contract Out Different Aspects of Operations, by Mode

	Heavy and light rail (N=7)	Fixed-route bus (N=167)	Demand response (N=133)	ADA paratransit (N=204)	Commuter rail (N=19)
Operations	71%	96%	97%	97%	95%
Maintenance	71	83	78	75	89
Security	57	31	24	26	58
Administrative services	43	72	72	73	63
Vehicles	29	26	47	40	37
Other	14	11	9	11	21

Source: GAO survey, April 2013.

Note: Responses do not add to one hundred percent because agencies were able to select more than one category. The other category includes scheduling, dispatching, reservations, ticketing, grant management services, and training. Heavy and light rail are combined due to the small number of agencies providing this service and similarities between the modes.

As shown in table 1, in each of the modes, less than half of the agencies that contract out include vehicles in their contracts. In our interviews with transit agencies and contractors, officials told us that transit agencies generally provide their own vehicles for several reasons:

- Owning vehicles gives the agency more flexibility to terminate a contract if needed, because it can be very difficult for an agency to quickly find another contractor with vehicles to provide continuous service.

- Purchasing and owning vehicles used in the transit service can attract bidders who would otherwise be hesitant to buy expensive vehicles without the assurance that they would be used beyond the initial length of the contract.

- Owning the vehicles gives the agency more control in making decisions about vehicle replacement or major repairs, such as replacing engines or transmissions. This can lower costs because the contractor may anticipate and budget for these costs in a contract without knowing for certain if they will be needed, in order to minimize their own risk.

Reasons for Contracting Decisions

According to our survey, the factors that transit agencies considered when deciding to contract a particular mode of service vary based on the mode and by needs of individual transit agencies. (See table 2.)

- For fixed-route bus, demand response, and paratransit service, the factors that were considered most often were reducing costs and improving efficiency.

- For commuter rail, the factors that were considered most often were starting new service and improving efficiency.

- For heavy and light rail, the factors that were considered most often were starting new service and being directed to contract by the Board of Directors.

Table 2: Top Factors Considered by Transit Agencies when Deciding to Contract Service, by Mode

	Heavy and light rail (N=6)	Fixed-route bus (N=160)	Demand response (N=122)	ADA paratransit (N=200)	Commuter rail (N=18)
To reduce costs	33%	68%	70%	74%	39%
Starting new service	67	43	41	33	83
To improve efficiency	33	61	58	59	56
To allow for more flexible service	33	41	54	46	44
Directed to contract by Board of Directors	50	23	20	23	44
To provide higher quality service	33	36	44	38	44

Source: GAO survey, April 2013.

Note: This table lists the categories with the highest percent of responses. Other potential responses with lower percentage of responses included expanding existing services; lack of availability of funding, equipment, or facilities to expand or start service; federal funds were available for contracting; and to meet state mandate or law. The table includes the responses of agencies that decided to contract out. Below we will discuss the top three reasons for contracting out service. Heavy and light rail are combined due to the small number of agencies providing this service and similarities between the modes.

Our literature review indicated these factors vary because needs and costs vary by mode, as well as the individual needs of transit agencies. Thus, for one transit agency, the cost of procuring vehicles and building facilities and expertise needed to operate the service may be a paramount concern, whereas it may be less of a concern for others. For example, commuter, heavy, and light rail services have high start-up costs because of the infrastructure and vehicles needed to operate the service, and, as supported by our survey results, starting new service is a primary factor in their decision to contract out for service. For fixed-route bus, demand response, and paratransit services, the start up costs are typically much lower. As a result, transit agencies may place more importance on reducing costs or providing more efficient service when making the decision to contract out for service.

Reducing costs. Although the factors that affect the decision to contract vary across modes, reducing costs is consistently taken into account, according to our survey, interviews, and literature review. The previous table shows that among our survey respondents that contract out, reducing cost was the most often cited factor. This finding was supported by our interviews with transit agency officials and the literature, which indicated that wage rates are lower for contracted drivers and operators, in part because:

- Contractors can "reset" wage rates to the market rate by hiring new operators at entry-level wage rates, according to some contractors we interviewed.

- Contractors may not always provide pensions and other benefits for contract workers.

- Contractors may have lower health insurance rates for their employees because of the large number of employees under their coverage.

As we will describe later in this report, unions have concerns regarding the lower wages and benefits for contract workers.

Some agencies, such as the Washington Metropolitan Area Transit Authority (Washington, D.C.) and the Metropolitan Rail Authority (Metra) (Chicago, Illinois), have found it more cost effective to contract out a portion of their services. Officials from the Washington Metropolitan Area Transit Authority told us that it is more cost effective for contractors to provide ADA paratransit service because of their reduced labor costs.

Officials at Metra said they would not achieve cost savings by directly operating two of their commuter rail services currently contracted out to the Burlington Northern/Santa Fe and Union Pacific Railroads. Officials stated that first, the freight railroads own the track and they would not be able to negotiate new track agreements with the railroads that would produce any more cost savings than what is in their present agreement. Second, they gain efficiencies from sharing certain overheads such as management personnel and facilities. If Metra had to create separate standalone facilities and staffing, this would be more expensive. Third, if Metra directly operated the service, then both Burlington Northern/Santa Fe and Union Pacific Railroad employees would be brought under Metra's collective bargaining agreements, which pay a higher wage rate than the freight railroads.

Starting new service. According to survey respondents as well as transit agency officials and contractors that we interviewed, transit agencies may contract out in order to avoid high start-up costs, including the cost of new services, procuring new vehicles, hiring staff, and obtaining facilities. For example, officials from the Nashville Regional Transportation Authority (Nashville, Tennessee) told us that they contract their commuter rail service because they lacked facilities to house or maintain their vehicles. Also, contracting out services can enable agencies to offer services they would otherwise not be able to provide—such as service that is located away from their main service area—because it is not cost effective. For example, while New Jersey Transit directly operates some of its services including fixed-route bus service, officials said when they create new services or expand other services it makes more sense for them to contract out, particularly in areas that lack a service garage or where there would be long travel times to where drivers store their vehicles at the end of the day.

In addition, from our interviews, we found that some transit agencies contract out when starting new service because they do not have the capability to perform transit services in-house. For example:

- New Orleans Regional Transit Authority (New Orleans, Louisiana) entered into a 10-year delegated management contract with a contractor that covers all planning, operations, and maintenance to quickly restore and rebuild the transit services and infrastructure that hurricane Katrina destroyed.

- Yuma County Intergovernmental Public Transportation Authority (Yuma, Arizona) contracts out all operations and maintenance for both its fixed-route bus and ADA paratransit services because it has only been in existence a short time and has not developed the capability to perform these services in house.

Improved efficiency and flexibility: According to our survey, improved efficiency and flexibility are two other primary considerations for contracting out service. Contractors and transit agency officials that we interviewed said that in some cases, contractors can operate more efficiently by having operators split their time between transit during the peak hours and other services, such as charter services—which are not typically provided by transit agencies—during other times of the day. Also, contractors may be able to provide service at a lower cost because their workforce is more flexible, with a greater number of employees working in part-time positions, resulting in decreased wage and benefit costs. According to one contractor we interviewed, offering part-time employment or flexible schedules may be also preferable for some employees.

Other factors. Legislative requirements that mandate or limit a transit agency from using a certain level of contracting, is another reason that can influence certain agencies' decisions to contract out service. However, state laws were not a leading factor in contracting decision-making, according to our survey respondents and seven transit agency officials that we interviewed.[8] For example, the state of Colorado limits the amount of contracting used by the Denver Regional Transit District (Denver, Colorado) to 58 percent. According to agency officials whom we interviewed, the cap on contracting has not had much impact on the agency's contracted services, which are currently about 56 percent of their bus and ADA paratransit operations. At the federal level, as described previously, when existing transit service is contracted out, Section 13(c) protections may be triggered, including assurances of employment and priority of reemployment. At all nine of the transit agencies we interviewed that use contracting, transit agency officials said that provisions of Section 13(c) have not been a deterrent to contracting; however, some transit agencies that responded to our survey reported that challenges presented by Section 13(c) are a reason for not contracting out service.

---

[8]This was not cited as one of the top factors in our survey because only a limited number of states have such mandates, and only transit agencies in those states would cite this as a factor.

Agencies that do not contract out any transit services or that contract out some, but not all aspects of their operations, also do so for reasons that vary by mode. As shown in table 3, for all modes except commuter rail, the top three reasons to not contract are that the agency desired to maintain control over operations, found no reason to change from the transit agency providing service, or found contracting was not cost effective. For commuter rail services, cost effectiveness was not among the primary reasons transit agencies reported for not contracting out service.

Table 3: Of Transit Agencies That Do Not Contract Some or All Operations, Percentage That Reported Reasons for Not Contracting

	Heavy and light rail (N=26)	Fixed-route bus (N=272)	Demand response (N=100)	Paratransit (N=182)	Commuter rail (N=4)
Want to maintain control over operations	62%	67%	66%	61%	50%
No reason to change to contracting	31	56	50	46	50
Contracting was not found to be cost effective	27	28	26	33	0
Challenges presented by Section 13(c)	19	19	9	14	25
Contracting is not allowed in union contract	15	20	4	11	25

Source: GAO survey, April 2013.

Note: The transit agencies whose responses are represented in the table are the survey respondents that did not contract out for any services or that do not contract out for some portion of their services. The responses do not add to 100 percent because agencies had the option of selecting more than one reason. Heavy and light rail are combined due to the small number of agencies providing this service and similarities between the modes.

Of the transit agencies that we interviewed, one transit agency does not contract out for any service and five transit agencies only contract out some modes, and they cited similar reasons as our survey respondents for their decisions not to contract out service. One transit agency that we interviewed that did not contract out any service—Western Maine Transportation Service (Auburn, Maine)—said that they never considered contracting. Transit agency officials stated that this was due in part to difficulty in finding a contractor willing to implement a costly drug and alcohol program that met FTA standards and also because the cost to contract out maintenance services would have been more expensive than directly operating it themselves, according to a comparative analysis performed by the transit agency of the cost to contract out versus the cost of operating it themselves. In addition, one transit agency contracted out service in the past and decided to bring the service back in-house. Dallas Area Rapid Transit (Dallas, Texas) used to use a contractor for its fixed-route bus service and later decided to provide the service using transit agency staff because, according to officials, in addition to local economic conditions and declining sales tax revenues, the contractor was not meeting service requirements and key performance indicators for maintenance of transit agency-owned vehicles. More recently, beginning in fiscal year 2012, the agency decided to keep operation of certain bus routes in-house after an analysis determined that the agency's costs to operate the service were lower than the privately contracted options.

Transit Agencies Use Many Methods to Select and Oversee Contractors

Contractor Selection

According to our survey responses, transit agencies use several methods to select contractors. (See fig. 2.) The most common method (used by 200 transit agencies that responded to our question) is competition through a request for proposals, wherein the transit agency solicits offers for the service to be provided.

Fewer than 50 transit agencies that responded to our survey that use contracting use each of the following methods:

- orders under pre-existing contracts, [9]

- sole source or preferred vendors,

- exercising a contract option, [10] and

- selection from a list of preferred vendors.

---

[9]Some contracts permit customer agencies to place orders for goods and services when specific needs arise.

[10]To exercise an option means to use a provision in an existing contract to extend the term of that contract.

Figure 2: Of Transit Agencies That Contract, Number That Use Each Method for Selecting Contractors

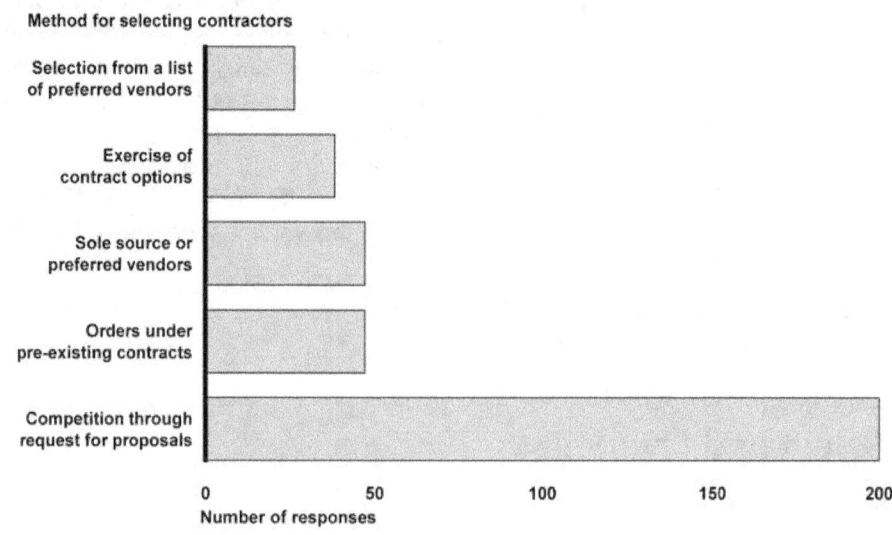

Source: GAO survey, April 2013.

Note: "Exercise of contract options" was not listed as a potential survey response. "Other" was listed as a survey response with the option to write in a response, and 38 respondents indicated that they exercised a contract option.

Officials we interviewed at eight of the nine transit agencies that use contracting said that they had at least three offers in response to their most recent solicitations for each mode operated, except when obtaining offers for the operation of their commuter rail services. Officials noted that it might not be cost effective for other contractors to make an offer on some commuter rail contracts because of specific circumstances, such as one contractor owning the tracks.

In selecting a contractor, transit agencies may be required to consider potential conflicts of interest. Nearly all (99 percent) of the agencies that we surveyed that use contracting have an ethics policy or standards in place that prohibit conflicts of interest. Furthermore, nearly all (99 percent) consider federal law, regulations, and guidance prohibiting conflicts of interest for contractor employees and businesses when contracting out.

Once the transit agency makes the decision to contract and selects a contractor, the two parties enter into a contract. Among other things, the contract specifies compensation, which can be structured in several ways. It may specify fixed-price compensation, which is based on a set price. For example, the payment may be a fixed amount per month. Compensation can also be hourly, so that the contractor pays based on the number of hours that the service is provided, which can be for the number of hours when the transit service is collecting fares or from the time the vehicles leave the facility until they return. Finally, the contractor can be compensated on a per-trip or per-mile basis, wherein the transit agency pays based on the number of trips provided or miles travelled. According to our survey, transit agencies structure compensation in their contract in various ways, including fixed price, price per revenue service based on hours or miles, price per vehicle miles or hours, and number of passenger trips provided. Contracts also specify the terms of service. For transit agencies that we interviewed, the most common contract term—used by six of the nine transit agencies that use contracting—was a 5-year initial contract period, sometimes including the option to extend into additional years. With respect to public access to contracts, federal regulations require transit agencies that enter into contracts using FTA grants to use their own procurement procedures that reflect applicable state and local laws and regulations.[11] Of the transit agencies that responded to our survey that contract out, 92 percent allow public access to all of their contract documents, 6 percent allow public access to some of their contract documents, and 1 percent do not allow public access to any of their documents.[12]

Contractor Oversight

Transit agencies reported undertaking a variety of activities to assess the quality of contracted services. Among our survey respondents that contract out services, the most commonly used methods are periodic reports or meetings, on-site inspections, the use of performance metrics, and real time monitoring. (See fig. 3.) About 84 percent of the surveyed transit agencies that contract out services reported having a specific unit or department to conduct oversight.

---

[11]49 C.F.R. § 18.36(b)(1).

[12]Percentages do not add to 100 due to rounding.

Figure 3: Of Transit Agencies That Contract, Number That Use Each Method for Assessing Quality of Contracted Services

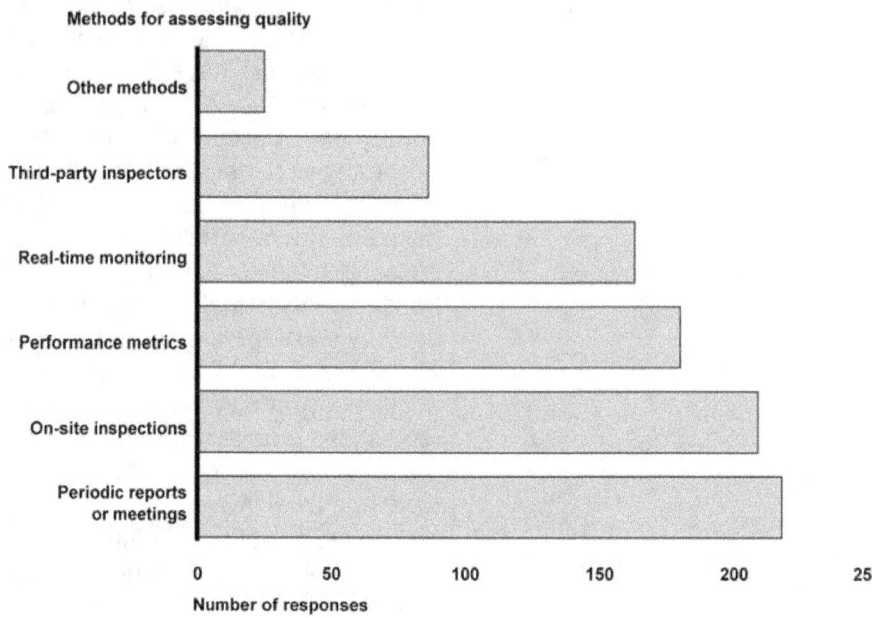

Source: GAO survey, April 2013.

Note: Agencies could select more than one category.

Transit agency officials whom we interviewed described how they use various methods, arrangements, and metrics they use to oversee contractor performance. For example:

- Officials at all of the nine agencies that use contractors told us that they oversee contractors' performance through activities such as routinely communicating with their contractors, either through periodic meetings or on as needed basis; inspecting contractors' facilities or vehicles; and/or using real-time monitoring devices installed on vehicles.

- Seven of the nine agencies use in-house staff to monitor the contractor's performance, while two use third-party contractors to perform this function. For example, in March 2013, the Washington Metropolitan Area Transit Authority signed a contract with a company to oversee the performance of the three transit contractors that operate its ADA paratransit services. Officials told us that using contractors to oversee the day-to-day performance of the contractors frees up in-house staff for more high-level oversight and management.

- Seven of the nine agencies that contract out for some or all of their transit services use metrics to establish performance incentives and/or penalties in contracts. For example, the Denver Regional Transit District uses a set of performance metrics, such as on-time performance and the number of complaints received from customers to measure the contractor's performance for its fixed-route bus service. The performance metrics are used to determine performance incentives or penalties. Likewise, officials from the New Orleans Regional Transit Authority said that they include performance incentives and penalties in their delegated management contract. Among the contract's provisions is a requirement for the contractor to reduce costs by 25 percent (adjusted for inflation) within 5 years in order to receive an automatic extension. The contractor said that it has already met this goal by focusing on safety throughout the organization, a focus that has reduced claim costs and related expenditures. Also, the contractor has changed the maintenance procedures and fleet operations and better managed the inventory of parts, which have also enhanced cost efficiencies. According to the contractor, during this 5-year period it has experienced increased service and ridership levels while meeting its cost-reduction goals. Conversely, officials from Yuma County Intergovernmental Public Transportation Authority do not include performance incentives in their contracts because they expect the contractor to always perform at a high level of service; however, they do have penalties for certain violations such as accidents.

Transit Agencies and Contractors Cite a Mix of Benefits and Challenges of Contracting; Unions Primarily Note Disadvantages

Transit Agencies' Views

Transit agency officials whom we interviewed and the literature we reviewed cite potential benefits to contracting for transit agencies, which may vary based on the needs and circumstances of individual transit agencies.

- *Contracting can be used to start or expand service.* According to our literature review, transit agencies view contracting as advantageous when new services need to be established quickly, based on the assumption that private firms can mobilize faster than a public agency.[13] Also, we have previously mentioned that starting new service is a primary consideration for contracting out service, according to our survey respondents (see table 2). Transit agencies contract out for new services in order to avoid the high start-up costs, including the cost of new services, procuring new vehicles, hiring staff, and obtaining facilities, according to transit agency officials that we interviewed. In addition, a 2005 study found that transit agencies use contracting to try out new service, as one agency did to provide new lines in outlying areas, because managers suspected that those new lines would have very low ridership and would not be cost effective. That study indicated that, according to the manager, contracting was more efficient because the contractor used smaller vehicles and had lower labor costs than the transit agency.[14]

- *Contracting can be used to maintain service levels.* According to our survey respondents' write-in answers on how transit service contracting has met their expectations, three transit agencies reported that contracting for certain services has allowed the transit agency to maintain service that would have been discontinued due to budget reductions. For example, one transit agency that contracts out its paratransit service with a ridership of about 52,000 per month reported that this service would have been cut due to cost constraints were it not for contracting.

- *Provides access to contractor's expertise and resources.* Two of the 10 transit agency officials whom we interviewed contract to gain the expertise and the resources that a contractor can bring to their transit

---

[13]Martin Wachs, Karen Trapenberg Frick, and Brian Taylor, *Contracting for Public Transit Services in the US: Evaluating the Tradeoffs*, in OECD/ITF, Privatisation and Regulation of Urban Transit Systems, OECD Publishing (2008).

[14]Hiroyuki Iseki, Amy Ford, and Rachel J. Factor, "Contracting Practice in Fixed-Route Transit Service: Case Studies in California," *Transportation Research Record: Journal of the Transportation Research Board*, 1927 (2005).

operation. For example, according to New Orleans Regional Transit Authority officials, the agency used a contractor because the officials felt that the contractor had the expertise and experience to lead the agency back to full recovery after Hurricane Katrina.

- *Shifts risk of providing service to contractor.* According to a 2007 study, when contracting for operation of services requiring buses, the transit industry has moved toward providing the vehicles and even the maintenance facility to a contractor.[15] As a result, the contractor assumes greater financial risk in terms of providing the insurance that is required for the vehicles. Transit agency officials we spoke with cited this transfer of risk as a benefit. For example, an official at Yuma County Intergovernmental Public Transportation Authority told us that contracting reduced the transit agency's insurance costs by 45 percent or more. Additionally, according to this official, insurance costs are typically higher for new transit authorities than for contractors, because they often do not have the same degree of experience operating transit services.

In addition to these reported benefits and their associated cost savings, transit agencies and literature cite the following challenges to contracting out transit services, which may, in some cases, outweigh the benefits or cost savings:

- *Diminishes an agency's direct control over operations.* Based on studies of contracting, some transit agencies have not accepted contracting because it does not provide an economic benefit equal to the risks associated with delegating service control to a contractor.[16] Specifically, according to this 2008 study, absent a compelling economic return that includes discounted future savings, in-house delivery of transit services is preferable because it provides managers with a direct line of authority to adjust services to meet a community's demand for services or deal with unforeseen service events.

---

[15]Jeffrey C. Arndt and Linda K. Cherrington, *The Role of Private-for-Hire Vehicles in Texas Public Transit,* Texas Transportation Institute, The Texas A&M University System (2007).

[16]See for example, Roland Zullo, "Transit contracting reexamined: determinants of cost efficiency and resource allocation," *Journal of Public Administration Research and Theory,* (2008).

- *Requires a complex request for proposal and contract-monitoring process.* Officials at two transit agencies told us that the contracting process is complex, long, and arduous. For example, officials from the Denver Regional Transportation District told us that they start the contract solicitation process approximately one year prior to the expiration of the existing contract. The process includes writing the scope of work, updating requirements (which includes getting input from various departments within the agency), issuing the request for proposal, evaluating the responses, negotiating with the selected contractor, and monitoring any start-up activities, thus costing the agency time and money. In addition, studies suggest that the costs of monitoring the contractor's performance may, in some cases, outweigh the benefits. In particular, a recent study found that transit agencies may need to keep in-house staff to evaluate and monitor contracts, which can reduce efficiency gains and related cost savings.[17] Another study suggests that the transaction costs that transit agencies incur when they draw up requests for proposals, evaluate offers, negotiate contracts, and monitor contracts with private providers could offset or even exceed cost savings from contracting transit service operation and management functions.[18]

- *Requires transit agency to address labor issues.* According to one study, transit agencies that are unionized must consider how organized labor would react to a contracting decision.[19] This study suggests that transit agencies face opposition to contracting from unions representing their employees. While a union may concede to contracting out new services, it tends to show much stronger opposition to contracting out existing services, which threatens union members' current jobs. However, according to the study, while most agencies with some in-house service are sensitive to union resistance to contracting, they may also face financial distress and must find ways to increase cost efficiency. Under such conditions, agencies need to maintain a good relationship and open communication with the union. This situation enables both parties to work together to

---

[17]Suzanne Leland and Olga Smirnova, "Understanding Local Government's Decision to Contract Out for Transit," paper prepared for the Association for Budgeting and Financial Management Meeting, Washington, D.C. (2009).

[18]Hiroyuki Iseki, "Effects of contracting on cost efficiency in U.S. fixed-route bus transit service," *Transportation Research Part A: Policy and Practice*, 44 (2010).

[19]Iseki, Ford, and Factor, "Contracting Practice," 88.

simultaneously increase the cost efficiency of the in-house service while avoiding significant job losses due to contracting. Even when transit managers are aware of other strategies for increasing cost efficiency, they need cooperation and concessions from the union to implement them.

Contractors' Views

Contractors we interviewed cited the following benefits to contracting.

- *Provides cost savings.* Contractors told us that they are able to increase efficiencies while reducing costs to transit agencies. For example, one contractor told us that his company includes in its contracts with transit agencies technology for routing and scheduling that is proprietary and, therefore, not available to transit agencies outside of a contract. Another contractor told us that its contracts provide access to specialized routing technology, which transit agencies would otherwise have to spend a great deal of money to purchase. Also, according to another contractor, providing the insurance on the vehicles that it uses can be a significant savings depending on the size of the transit agency. As previously mentioned in this report, contracting can also be a way for transit agencies to potentially lower their health insurance costs. For example, contractors with large numbers of employees may have lower health insurance rates and be able to offer lower rates to their employees. As a result of these and other efficiencies, one contractor told us that if it were to exclude the cost of capital assets (vehicles and facilities) the operating costs for the contractor would be significantly lower, usually in the range of 15 percent to 35 percent. However, expected cost savings do not always come to fruition. For example, based on anecdotal evidence from our literature review, one transit agency brought transit services back in house after it found that its arrangement with its contractor was too expensive. The contractor had a 5-year contract that was terminated in less than 3 years.

- *Provides access to contractor's expertise and resources.* Contractors also cited the expertise and resources that they can bring to a transit agency as a benefit to contracting. One contractor we interviewed told us that it brings specific knowledge and expertise in areas such as training, and resources, such as customer call centers, and thus allows the transit agency to focus on its own or management strengths. Additionally, another contractor told us that contracting allows a private company to provide resources that the transit agency does not have. For example, transit agencies might receive access to expertise for technical issues and labor negotiations, as well as discounted purchasing rates for fuel, vehicle parts, and other equipment, because of the large amount purchased by the contractor to cover several transit agencies' operations.

- *Increases labor flexibility.* Contractors cited labor flexibility as a benefit to contracting. For example, according to one contractor, contracting offers the transit agency more labor flexibility, in that, if additional staff is needed to perform a particular service the contractor generally has greater flexibility to quickly bring in the needed staff, because it has the resources of the entire company, whereas the transit agency may be limited in that regard. Another contractor said that its company's labor agreements are not very restrictive in terms of how the workforce is deployed or scheduled. For example, the contractor can cross-train staff, and if a dispatcher is needed to drive or a driver is needed to perform dispatching functions, its labor agreements generally allow those things to happen, which increases efficiencies.

The contractors we interviewed cited few challenges to contracting. Three of the six contractors we spoke to said that the capital investment that is required for a contract might prevent them from bidding. Also, according to one contractor, the biggest barrier that exists to contracting is transit agency funds. Transit agencies are sometimes forced into a contracting arrangement based on price rather than value because of funding constraints.

Union Views

Officials at national and local unions we spoke with said that whereas contracting may provide some short-term cost savings to transit agencies, the savings are almost entirely from lower wages and benefits paid by the private companies to their employees. This statement is consistent with what we heard from some transit agencies regarding the source of cost savings associated with contracting. Recent studies we reviewed also suggest that this is the case. For example, one study of 12 transit agencies found that cost savings accrue primarily as a result of private transit labor consistently earning lower wages and fewer benefits compared to similar public sector employees.[20] Moreover, one local union official that we spoke with told us that the wages for the transit-agency bus operators it represents are generally higher than the contractors' bus operators' wages. A new bus driver starts at about $12-13 per hour for

---

[20]Wachs, Trapenberg, and Taylor, *Contracting for Public,* 57-58.

the contractors and $15 per hour for that transit agency, according to that union official. Additionally, this union official told us that while wages for contractor employees and transit agency employees tend to be at the same level at the top of the pay scale, it takes contractor employees longer to reach the top levels. However, according to national union officials, commuter rail employees covered under the Railway Labor Act receive comparable wages and benefits whether employed by transit agencies or contractors.

The national and local union officials we interviewed stated that contracting might lead to decreased level of safety, poor service quality, and hidden costs.

- *Decreased level of safety.* Local union officials we spoke with said that contracting decreases the level of safety, possibly because, in their view, contracted employees receive less training than transit agency employees. For example, one local union official told us that the local transit agency provides 8 weeks of classroom and on-the-road training whereas the contractors provide 5 weeks of training. Another local union official told us that the contractor reduced its training course to 2 weeks from 3 (the amount provided by the transit agency). In addition, one union official told us that privatized buses are not as safe as agency buses. For example, the official said that he had seen private buses on the road with side view mirrors held in place with duct tape. Two studies published since 2002 discussed the quality of contracted services, and one noted that contracted service had higher rates (by 70 percent) of vehicle collisions and the other reported that service quality may be lower among low cost contracted operators.[21] However, as previously mentioned in this report, officials at all of the nine agencies we interviewed that use contractors told us that they oversee contractors' performance through various activities, including inspecting contractors' facilities or vehicles, and none of the officials that we interviewed raised concerns about safety. Additionally, one transit agency told us that officials inspect the contractors' buses on a daily basis to determine their condition or whether preventive maintenance or repairs have been performed. The agency also reviews performance data related to customer complaints, on-time performance, accidents, and maintenance, which it compiles in a monthly performance report.

---

[21]Wachs, Trapenberg, and Taylor, *Contracting for Public,* 57. Collision data are from a sample of approximately 320 transit agencies.

- *Poor service quality.* Union officials we spoke with generally agreed that because contractors are profit driven, they may not have incentives to provide the same level and quality of service as the transit agencies. According to one union official, the contractor will only provide the level of effort mandated by the contract, whereas the agency will go above and beyond to ensure high-quality service. Recent literature has discussed the quality of contracted services, with one study finding that contracted service had more vehicle breakdowns (by 36 percent).[22] Anecdotal evidence from the literature shows that some contractors are having difficulties in providing quality service. For example, a contractor took over paratransit operations in a Florida county in the summer of 2012, and by May 2013, due to performance failures, such as vehicle breakdowns, accidents, maintenance requirements, and other problems; the county fined the contractor $2.2 million. The county has since directed the transit agency to find a second service provider by November 2013, to help provide paratransit services. Also, as discussed earlier, one transit agency that we interviewed ceased using a contractor for its fixed-route bus service because of concerns about service quality, among other issues. However, one union representative we spoke with thought that the quality of service may actually be better under a contractor, because contractors are penalized for not meeting performance measures, such as on-time performance, as discussed earlier in this report.

- *Hidden costs.* Union officials cited hidden costs incurred by transit agencies related to activities such as proposal evaluation and contract monitoring as a disadvantage to contracting. As previously mentioned in this report, transaction costs that public agencies incur when they draw up requests for proposals, evaluate offers, negotiate contracts, and, monitor contracts with private providers could offset or even exceed cost savings from contracting transit service operation and management functions. Moreover, one local union official we spoke with told us that privatization adds a level of management, which can create inefficiencies and duplication of effort. For example, he told us that one transit agency that he represents has two sets of street supervisors—one for the contractor and another for the transit agency—each doing the same work. Also, if a private contractor fails

---

[22]Wachs, Trapenberg, and Taylor, *Contracting for Public,* 57.

to provide service on a route, the transit agency is ultimately responsible and must find other means to operate the route.

Riders' Views

According to our interviews with five of the six citizens' advisory groups that are affiliated with transit agencies, the quality of service was generally viewed as being comparable whether provided by the transit agency or a contractor. The Denver Regional Transit District conducted a customer satisfaction survey and found no measurable difference in customer satisfaction between in-house and contracted services. In addition, Dallas Area Rapid Transit citizens' advisory group said that the level of service has been good with contracting. Lastly, the advisory board for Metropolitan Rail Authority told us that the public generally does not know whether a contractor or the transit agency operates services.

Concluding Observations

Contracting is not a one-size-fits-all approach for providing transit services. For some transit agencies, contracting may be the most cost-effective way to provide service, because transit agencies can benefit from access to certain technologies or reduced labor, fuel, and insurance costs. For other transit agencies, contracting may be impractical because of additional costs incurred from the bidding process and contractor oversight. Given our challenging economy, it is important that transit agencies are able to make decisions that allow them to use federal funds in the most efficient manner while also considering factors such as providing high quality service, regardless of whether these services are provided by transit agency employees or contractors.

Agency Comments

We provided a copy of this report to the Department of Transportation and the Department of Labor for review. The agencies had no comment on the report.

We are sending copies of this report to interested congressional committees, the Secretary of the Department of Transportation, and the Secretary of the Department of Labor. In addition, this report will be available at no charge on GAO's web site at http://www.gao.gov.

If you or your staff have any questions or would like to discuss this work, please contact me at (202) 512-2834 or wised@gao.gov. Contact points for our Offices of Congressional Relations and Public Affairs may be found on the last page of this report. Individuals making key contributions to this report are listed in appendix II.

David J. Wise
Director, Physical Infrastructure Issues

Appendix I: Objectives, Scope, and Methodology

To comply with the Moving Ahead for Progress in the 21st Century Act (MAP-21) mandate we addressed the following questions: (1) What is the extent that transit agencies contract public transit operations and services and identify reasons for doing so? (2) What methods do transit agencies use to select and oversee contracted services? (3) What are the potential benefits, challenges, and disadvantages of contracting out public transit operations and other services?

To address our questions, we conducted a web-based survey of all 637 transit agencies that reported to the Federal Transit Administration's (FTA) National Transit Database in 2011 and operate fixed-route bus; demand response; ADA (Americans with Disability Act) paratransit; and heavy, light, or commuter rail services and asked about their contracting practices in 2011. We excluded transit agencies that received a reporting waiver. The survey was conducted from March 4, 2013, to April 23, 2013. To prepare the questionnaire, we pretested potential questions with transit agencies of different sizes and that operate all of the modes to ensure that (1) the questions and possible responses were clear and thorough, (2) terminology was used correctly, (3) questions did not place an undue burden on the respondents, (4) the information was feasible to obtain, and (5) the questionnaire was comprehensive and unbiased. On the basis of feedback from the four pretests we conducted, we made changes to the content and format of some survey questions. The results of our survey can be found at GAO-13-824SP.

To identify transit agencies to survey, we conducted interviews with the appropriate FTA officials responsible for the National Transit Database to learn about information collected from transit agencies regarding transit contracting and obtain contact information. We contacted all of the transit agencies in advance, by e-mail, to ensure that we had identified the correct respondents and to request their completion of the questionnaire. After the survey had been available for 1 week, and again after 2 and 4 weeks, we used e-mail and telephone calls to contact transit agencies who had not completed their questionnaires. Using these procedures, we received responses from 463 transit agencies for a response rate of 73 percent. The results of our survey are not generalizeable to all transit agencies. Estimates and responses to survey questions in this report refer only to the views of the respondents. The survey was a census survey, and we did not try to extrapolate the findings to the agencies that chose not to respond. Because this was not a sample survey, there are no sampling errors. However, the practical difficulties of conducting any survey may introduce errors, commonly referred to as nonsampling errors. For example, difficulties in how a particular question is interpreted, in the sources of information that are available to respondents, or in how the data are entered into a database or were analyzed can introduce unwanted variability into the survey results. We took steps in the development of the questionnaire, the data collection, and the data analysis to minimize these nonsampling errors. For instance, a survey specialist designed the questionnaire in collaboration with GAO staff who have subject-matter expertise. Further, the draft questionnaire was pretested with four transit agencies to ensure that the questions were relevant, clearly stated, and easy to comprehend. When the data were analyzed, a second, independent analyst checked all computer programs. Finally, we analyzed nonresponding transit agencies for evidence of bias. We found that transit agencies that provide heavy rail were less likely to respond to our survey than other transit agencies.[1]

To obtain in-depth information and contracting experiences from local jurisdictions, we interviewed transit agencies at ten sites across the country. (See table 4.) At each location, we attempted to interview private transit contractors, citizens' advisory groups, and a local union. We judgmentally selected these locations based on geographic location, population served, transit modes, agency sizes, and contracting practices. The interviews from these locations are not generalizable to all transit agencies.

Table 4: Transit Agencies, Contractors, Local Unions, and Citizens Advisory Groups Interviewed by Location

Location	Transit agency	Contractor[a]	Local union[b]	Citizens advisory group[c]
Auburn, Maine	Western Maine Transportation Service	None	None	None
Bourbonnais, Illinois	River Valley Metro Mass Transit District	First Transit	Amalgamated Transit Union (ATU) Local 1745	None
Chicago, Illinois	Chicago Metropolitan Rail Authority (METRA)	None	None	Citizens Advisory Board
Dallas, Texas	Dallas Area Rapid Transit (DART)	MV Transportation	ATU Local 1338	DART Citizens Advisory Committee

[1]Among other things, MAP-21 required us to report on the size of populations served by contracted services and the extent of unionization among contracted employees. We included questions in our survey; however, we found the responses to these questions to be unreliable due to the large number of transit agencies that did not provide this information or selected "don't know" as a response.

Location	Transit agency	Contractor[a]	Local Union[b]	Citizens advisory group[c]
Denver, Colorado	Denver Regional Transportation District (RTD)	First Transit	ATU Local 1001	RTD Customer Panel
Nashville, Tennessee	Nashville Regional Transportation Authority (RTA)	Transit Solutions Group	ATU Local 1235	None
Newark, New Jersey	New Jersey Transit	Twenty-First Century Rail Corporation	Transport Workers Union (TWU) International Representative on behalf of TWU Local 229	North Jersey Transit Advisory Committee, South Jersey Transit Advisory Committee, and Senior Citizens & Disabled Resident Transportation Advisory Committee
New Orleans, Louisiana	New Orleans Regional Transit Authority	Veolia	None	Special Transit Services Committee
Washington, D.C.	Washington Metropolitan Area Transit Authority (WMATA)	Diamond Transport	None	WMATA Accessibility Advisory Committee
Yuma, Arizona	Yuma County Intergovernmental Transportation Authority	First Transit	ATU Local 1433	None

Source: GAO.

[a]If we obtained a national perspective on contracting from a contractor in one location, we did not interview officials affiliated with the same contractor at other sites we visited. In one location, we did not interview the contractor because the transit agency contracts with freight railroads to operate and maintain the service.

[b]In some locations, the local union representative did not return our phone calls to set up interviews or did not wish to be interviewed. In one location, we did not interview the local union because the transit agency does not contract and in another location we did not interview the local union because we gathered commuter rail union perspectives at the national level.

[c]Some locations did not have an active citizens' advisory group.

We also interviewed the American Public Transportation Association, Community Transportation Association of America, and national labor unions representing operators and maintenance workers including the American Federation of Labor and Congress of Industrial Organizations, the Amalgamated Transit Union and the Transport Workers Union, International Brotherhood of Teamsters, and representatives of the following unions for commuter rail operators and maintenance workers— International Brotherhood of Electrical Workers, Brotherhood of Railroad Signalmen, National Conference of Firemen & Oilers, Brotherhood of Maintenance of Way Employees Division, Sheet Metal Air, Rail and Transportation - Sheet Metal Workers' International Association, Transport Workers Union, Transportation Trades Department, International Association of Machinists, Sheet Metal Air, Rail and Transportation-United Transportation Union, and the Brotherhood of Locomotive Engineers and Trainmen. We also interviewed Federal

Railroad Administration officials regarding contracting of commuter services and Department of Labor officials to understand their role when transit agencies decide to contract out services.

We also reviewed and synthesized information from our body of work and relevant literature on contracting out transit services in the United States. We reviewed citations identified through a search of databases containing peer-reviewed articles, government reports, and "gray literature," including Transport Research International Documentation, Social SciSearch, and PROQUEST.[2] Publications were limited to the years after 2001. After an initial review of citations, 37 articles were selected for further review. To collect information on the articles, we developed a data collection instrument to gather information on the articles' scope and purpose, methods, findings and their limitations, and additional areas for follow-up, including a review of the bibliography to determine the completeness of our literature search. To apply this data collection instrument, one analyst reviewed each article and recorded information in the data collection instrument. A second analyst then reviewed each completed data collection instrument to verify the accuracy of the information recorded. We summarized the findings and limitations of the articles based on the completed data collection instruments, as well as areas for additional research identified in the articles.

We conducted this performance audit from October 2012 to September 2013 in accordance with generally accepted government auditing standards. Those standards require that we plan and perform the audit to obtain sufficient, appropriate evidence to provide a reasonable basis for our findings and conclusions based on our audit objectives. We believe that the evidence obtained provides a reasonable basis for our findings and conclusions based on our audit objectives.

---

[2]"Gray literature" publications may include, but are not limited to, the following types of materials: reports (pre-prints, preliminary progress and advanced reports, technical reports, statistical reports, memoranda, state-of-the art reports, market research reports, etc.), theses, conference proceedings, technical specifications and standards, noncommercial translations, bibliographies, technical and commercial documentation, and official documents not published commercially (primarily government reports and documents).

Appendix II: GAO Contact and Staff Acknowledgments

GAO Contact	David J. Wise, (202) 512-2834 or wised@gao.gov
Staff Acknowledgments	In addition to the contact named above, Teresa Spisak (Assistant Director), Stephanie Purcell, Carl Barden, Dwayne Curry, Leia Dickerson, Lorraine Ettaro, Kathy Gilhooly, Cathy Hurley, Stu Kaufman, Alex Lawrence, and Amy Rosewarne made key contributions to this report.